GERMAN TRACTION

Andrew Cole

AMBERLEY

First published 2018

Amberley Publishing
The Hill, Stroud
Gloucestershire, GL5 4EP

www.amberley-books.com

Copyright © Andrew Cole, 2018

ISBN 978 1 4456 6694 5 (print)
ISBN 978 1 4456 6695 2 (ebook)

British Library Cataloguing in Publication Data.
A catalogue record for this book is available from
the British Library.

Origination by Amberley Publishing.
Printed in the UK.

Introduction

With its central location in the heart of Europe, Germany has always been a very busy country for both passenger and freight services. The large size of the country also means that a large number of locomotives were required to run such services.

At the end of the Second World War, Germany was split into East and West Germany, and as such, both sides ordered their own locomotives. Upon reunification of the country in 1990, both of the two main operators, Deutsche Bundesbahn in the West and Deutsche Reichsbahn in the East, finally became one company in 1994, known as Deutsche Bahn (DB). One of the first actions was to renumber the locomotives into one common numbering system, while a repainting programme also got underway.

On the locomotive front, the joining of the two companies meant that there were thousands of locomotives in use, both on passenger and freight services. Since DB took over there have been many locomotive withdrawals, but also many new locomotives introduced.

This book concentrates on the locomotive scene in the present day since space constraints meant that a lot of the older locomotives had to be overlooked, as there are so many new types in traffic today.

Passenger workings in Germany are slowly being taken over by new-build EMUs and the InterCity-Express (ICE) network continues to evolve, but there are still plenty of loco-hauled services in the country. The main locomotives used are Classes 101, 111, 112, 114, 120, 143, 146, 182, 218 and 245, although large inroads are being made into the older series of locomotives. The Class 101 and 120 locomotives are used on the main InterCity routes and are seen all over the country.

The Class 111 locomotives can be found working around Cologne, Darmstadt, Dortmund, Düsseldorf, Frankfurt, Munich and Stuttgart. The Class 112 locomotives work out of Berlin, Cottbus, Dresden, Frankfurt, Magdeburg, Stuttgart, Halle and Hamburg. The Class 143s can be seen at Berlin, Cologne, Cottbus, Darmstadt, Dortmund, Dresden, Frankfurt, Halle and Nuremburg, while the Class 146 locomotives work out of Cologne, Darmstadt, Dortmund, Dresden, Düsseldorf, Frankfurt, Halle, Hamburg, Hannover, Leipzig, Magdeburg, Offenburg, Stuttgart and Ulm.

On the diesel front, the Class 218 locomotives work mainly out of Hamburg, Neibüll, Munich, Stuttgart and Ulm, while the new Class 245s work from Frankfurt, Neibüll Westerland, Munich, Stuttgart and Ulm, so there are many places to visit to catch some loco-hauled passenger workings.

There are just a small number of other passenger operators who use locomotives on their services. The most well-known is Metronom, who operate local services around Hamburg, using Class 146 and Class 246 TRAXX locomotives on their services, with the diesels working to Cuxhaven. The next well-known is Hamburg-Köln-Express (HKX), who operate between the two cities using hired-in Class 182 Taurus locomotives from Dispolok. They now run under the FlixTrain banner. Another well-known operator is Alex, who use Class 223 locomotives around the Munich area.

With Germany being so large, there are vast numbers of freight traffic throughout the whole country. The main classes that DB use are 140, 145, 151, 152, 155, 185, 186, 189, 232 and 247. Many of the newer built locomotives are able to work into neighbouring countries, helping to avoid time-consuming loco changes at the border. The most common locomotives used cross-border are the Class 185s, which can be seen working in Switzerland, Austria and also through to Denmark, among other countries. The large diesels used are the Class 232 'Ludmillas', which were built in the USSR during the 1970s, and the General Motors-built Class 247 locomotives.

There are also a large number of yard and trip locomotives that are still used in Germany, with the most common being the Class 290s, 294s, 295s and 298s. They are also supplemented by the newer Voith-built Gravita Class 261 and 265 locomotives. DB also have a sizeable fleet of shunting locomotives in use, the most notable being the Class 335, 362 and 363 locomotives, which are used throughout the country, with many of the larger yards and stations using more than one example.

Private operators also make up a large amount of freight traffic throughout Germany. The most common locomotives used are the Bombardier-built TRAXX Class 185 and 186 locomotives, which can be seen working the length and breadth of the country. Many of the locomotives used are leased through leasing company Dispolok, who use large numbers of Class 182 and 185 locomotives. The newest leasing company in Germany is European Locomotive Leasing, who have amassed a large fleet of Siemens-built Class 193 Vectron locomotives. These locos are hired out to many different operators, and they can also be used cross-border.

There are many different places to see large numbers of loco-hauled services, both passenger and freight, with most of the larger cities, including Hamburg, Hannover, Berlin, Bremen, Munich, Cologne and Düsseldorf seeing large numbers of freight moves throughout the day.

All in all, Germany is a fantastic place to visit, not only for loco-hauled passenger services, but also to see large amounts of freight traffic. It is a great place to start your European adventures, and is fully recommended. This book is split into national operator DB, followed by private operators, and includes locomotives found in Germany and also German-registered locomotives working in other European countries.

No. 101001, 24 July 2015

No. 101001 rounds the curve as it approaches Hamburg-Harburg station while at the head of a passenger working, consisting of a rake of single-deck carriages. 145 of these locomotives were built by Adtranz from 1996 onwards, all of which are still in use today.

No. 101006, 24 July 2015

No. 101006 is seen departing from Hamburg-Harburg while propelling a rake of single-deck InterCity carriages. This loco carries an advert for Swiss Travel Systems, which includes a view of Switzerland.

No. 101007, 23 July 2015

No. 101007 is seen under the impressive roof at Köln HBF. The Class 101 locomotives were built to replace the ageing Class 103 locomotives on many of the InterCity workings in Germany.

No. 101044, 23 July 2015

No. 101044 departs from Bremen HBF while propelling an InterCity working, but the external appearance of this loco leaves a lot to be desired. Bremen is an incredibly busy station for both passenger and freight workings, with many different operators passing through the station.

No. 101054, 24 July 2015

No. 101054 arrives at Hamburg-Harburg while propelling an InterCity working towards Hamburg HBF. This is another very busy station in Germany, with a large amount of freight traffic being generated by the docks, as well as a large amount of passenger services, both run by DB and private operator Metronom.

No. 101092, 21 July 2015

No. 101092 makes a station call at Köln HBF while on an InterCity working. This is another member of the class to carry an advert for Swiss Travel Systems, the smooth sides being ideal for adverts. This time the loco carries an image of the Bernina Express.

No. 101102, 24 July 2015

No. 101102 is seen at Hannover HBF while propelling an InterCity working. Over the years this class of locomotive have carried various overall advertising liveries, and No. 101102 is seen with one for Vedes, a German leisure retailer.

No. 101110, 22 July 2015

No. 101110 rolls through Köln West with an InterCity working heading for Köln HBF. This is another member of the class to carry an advertising livery, this time for the football club Eintracht Frankfurt. The loco is named the same.

No. 101114, 24 July 2015

No. 101114 arrives at Hamburg-Harburg with a rake of older DB single-deck carriages. This class of loco is popular for carrying advert liveries due to the fact they are seen in most areas of the country. No. 101114 carries an advert for Köln tourism.

No. 111011, 23 July 2015

No. 111011 is seen waiting to depart from Köln HBF coupled to a rake of double-deck DB Regio carriages. 227 of these locomotives were built from 1974 onwards by various manufacturers, and most are still in service, except for some accident victims.

No. 111096, 21 July 2015

No. 111096 arrives at Köln HBF with a rake of single-deck carriages. Despite the oldest members of this class being over forty years old, they are still giving sterling service on the DB network. The Class 111 locomotives based in Cologne work to Aachen Siegen.

No. 111124, 21 July 2015

No. 111124 is seen departing from Düsseldorf HBF with a DB Regio working. Not all locomotives carry the check digit on the front as No. 111124 does. The Class 111s based in Düsseldorf also work out to Aachen Siegen.

No. 111126, 22 July 2015

No. 111126, working in push-pull mode, makes a station call at Köln West while on a DB Regio working.

No. 111158, 20 February 2017

No. 111158 is seen waiting to depart from Wuppertal at the head of four double-deck DB Regio carriages. These locos operate in push-pull mode, with a driving trailer at the other end of the formation. (TC)

No. 112141, 24 July 2015

No. 112141 stands in front of the impressive station building at Hamburg HBF, having propelled its DB Regio working into the station. Ninety of the Class 112/1 locos were built in the 1990s.

No. 112143, 13 May 2016

No. 112143 departs from Hamburg HBF while propelling a rake of double-deck DB Regio carriages. Note the Hamburg S-Bahn unit arriving in the background. (TC)

No. 112151, 24 July 2015

No. 112151 is seen inside the impressive Hamburg HBF having arrived with a rake of double-deck DB Regio carriages. Note the 'Nah.sh' decal on the cabside, which is the main provider of information and tickets for use in the Hamburg area.

No. 112164, 21 July 2015

No. 112164 is seen arriving at Düsseldorf HBF at the head of a rake of double-deck DB Regio carriages. This was working in top-and-tail mode with classmate No. 112166 coupled at the other end, despite there being a driving trailer in the formation.

No. 120118, 24 July 2015

No. 120118 departs from Hamburg-Harburg while propelling an InterCity working. Sixty of these locomotives were built from 1987 onwards, and they followed a pre-production order of five locomotives. The Class 120 locomotives work InterCity services, and can be seen countrywide.

No. 120138, 22 July 2015

No. 120138 rolls through Köln West with a rake of single-deck carriages, with a driving trailer right behind the locomotive. A start has now been made on withdrawing these locomotives from service.

No. 120159, 24 July 2015

No. 120159 arrives at Hamburg-Harburg with a DB InterCity working. Note the addition of the tail lamp due to the defective tail light on the locomotive.

No. 120160, 22 February 2017

No. 120160 is seen at Rostock at the head of a short two-coach rail inspection train. This loco is painted yellow, as it is operated by the departmental sector, and it is the only Class 120 to carry this livery. (TC)

No. 140353, 22 July 2015

No. 140353 passes through Köln West while hauling No. 145023 light engine. This class of locomotive was manufactured in large numbers from 1957 onwards, with a total of 879 being built. Many have been withdrawn and scrapped, but a large number have found use with private operators.

No. 140569, 23 July 2015

No. 140569 is seen passing through Hannover Linden Fischerhof station with a rake of cargowaggons. This is a very busy station for freight traffic, with large marshalling yards located nearby.

No. 140680, 23 July 2015

No. 140680 departs from the large yard adjacent to Hannover Linden Fischerhof station with a rake of empty steel-carrying wagons. The Class 140 locomotives are slowly disappearing from the DB rosters.

No. 140833, 22 July 2015

No. 140833 pilots classmate No. 140837 through Köln West with an empty steel working. Of note are the two different pantographs used on the two locomotives. With the large number of locomotives built, this was the standard locomotive in use in Germany in the 1960s.

No. 143168, 21 July 2015

No. 143168 is seen at Köln HBF with a DB Regio service formed of a rake of double-deck carriages. There were 636 of these locomotives built for both East and West Germany from 1985 onwards by LEW. The Cologne-based Class 143 locomotives work on Mönchengladbach to Koblenz services.

No. 143568, 23 July 2015

No. 143568 is seen departing from Köln HBF with a DB Regio working. These locos were classified as Class 243s in East Germany and Class 143s in West Germany. Upon reunification, all locomotives were numbered as Class 143s.

No. 143651, 24 July 2015

No. 143651 is seen waiting to depart from Hannover HBF with a DB Regio working. This class is still used in large numbers on passenger workings, but their numbers are gradually being eroded.

No. 143930, 24 July 2015

No. 143930 is seen departing from Hamburg HBF with a DB Regio working. Some Class 143 locomotives have been rebuilt as Class 114 and have a higher maximum speed when compared to the Class 143 locomotives.

No. 145023, 22 July 2015

No. 145023 is seen being hauled light engine through Köln West by No. 140353. Adtranz built eighty of these locomotives from 1996 onwards, and they were the forerunners to the popular TRAXX class of locomotives, which are in use over most of Europe today.

No. 145047, 22 July 2015

No. 145047 runs light engine through Köln West. The German livery of red and grey has remained unchanged for many years, although the operator name has changed from DB Cargo to Railion, then DB Schenker, and finally back to DB Cargo.

No. 145054, 21 July 2015

No. 145054 is seen passing Düsseldorf-Rath with a rake of bogie oil tankers. This is another extremely busy station for freight traffic, with a constant procession throughout the day.

No. 145060, 24 July 2015

No. 145060 is seen passing Hamburg-Harburg with a container working that had originated from the nearby docks, and there is a large marshalling yard situated just beyond the station.

No. 145080, 21 July 2015

No. 145080 passes through Düsseldorf-Rath at the head of a mixed freight working. This was the last Class 145 locomotive built for DB, and it is looking a little scruffy when seen. The Class 145 locomotives are the freight version of this type of locomotive, with the Class 146s being the passenger version.

No. 146008, 23 July 2015

Carrying an advert for DB, No. 146008 is seen departing from Köln HBF while propelling a rake of double-deck DB Regio carriages. To date nearly 150 of these locomotives have been built in various batches. The Cologne-based Class 146 locomotives work to various places, including Minden, Munster, Düsseldorf and Hamm.

No. 146010, 22 July 2015

No. 146010 passes non-stop through Köln West with a DB Regio service consisting of six double-deck carriages. This was working towards Emmerich, as can be seen in the front destination indicator.

No. 146018, 21 July 2015

No. 146018 departs from Düsseldorf HBF with a DB Regio working to Koblenz. There were thirty-one Class 146/0 locomotives built for passenger workings, and at the time all were based at Dortmund.

No. 146026, 21 July 2015

No. 146026 arrives at Düsseldorf HBF with a DB Regio working to Emmerich. All of the Class 146 locomotives were built by Bombardier.

No. 146101, 23 July 2015

No. 146101 is seen making a station call at Bremen HBF with a DB Regio working to Osnabrück. Thirty-two Class 146/1 locomotives were built, again for passenger workings, with the different sub-classes denoting the different areas in which they work.

No. 146124, 24 July 2015

No. 146124 is seen running through Hamburg HBF while hauling just a single DB Regio double-deck driving trailer. Note the 'Not in Service' in the destination indicator.

No. 146127, 23 July 2015

No. 146127 is seen waiting to depart from Bremen HBF while propelling a DB Regio working. This locomotive carries an advert livery for the town of Marienhafe, located on the Emsland Line.

No. 146228, 9 September 2014

No. 146228 is seen at Basel Badischer Bahnhof, Switzerland, with a DB Regio working to Müllheim. This station is located inside Switzerland, but is operated by Deutsche Bahn. There are seventy-nine Class 146/2 locomotives.

No. 146555, 14 May 2016

No. 146555 is seen arriving at Köln HBF wearing the attractive reversed white livery. These are the newest Class 146 locomotives operated by DB. (TC)

No. 151002, 22 July 2015

No. 151002 passes through Köln West at the head of a ballast working. This class of locomotives were introduced from 1972 onwards, and were a replacement for the Class 150 locomotives.

No. 151031, 21 July 2015

No. 151031 is seen approaching Düsseldorf-Rath while double-heading with classmate No. 151076. Of note are the two different shades of red carried by both locomotives. 170 members of this class of locomotive were built by various builders.

No. 151094, 24 July 2015

No. 151094 passes Hamburg-Harburg while double-heading with classmate No. 151104 to haul an ore train, and the locomotives are dedicated to this use as they have been fitted with autocouplers. A start has been made on withdrawing these from DB use, with some passing to private operators.

No. 151106, 24 July 2015

No.151106 is seen at Hamburg-Harburg with an ore working. This loco is one of the class members fitted with autocouplers, which can be clearly seen, and is fitted with a yellow sticker adjacent to the buffers, indicating this modification.

No. 151153, 22 July 2015

No. 151153 is seen passing Köln West with an empty steel working. Note the windows on the side of the locomotive, which would make the interior very light to work in. This is a very busy station for passing freight traffic.

No. 152013, 22 July 2015

No. 152013 is seen passing through Köln West while hauling a rake of loaded intermodal wagons. The DB Class 152 locomotives are part of the Siemens ES 64 Eurosprinter class of locomotives.

No. 152053, 24 July 2015

No. 152053 passes Hamburg-Harburg with an intermodal working. A total of 170 Class 152 units were introduced from 1997 onwards for use on freight workings.

No. 152085, 21 July 2015

No. 152085 passes Düsseldorf-Rath at the head of a loaded automotive working, still carrying Railion logos; most have been removed by now, as they are operated by DB Cargo.

No. 152105, 23 July 2015

No. 152105 is seen passing Hannover Linden Fischerhof, while another freight working goes the other way. This class of locomotives shares the same internals as the Siemens Taurus locomotives.

No. 152165, 21 July 2015

No. 152165 is seen passing Düsseldorf-Rath with a loaded steel working. Of note is the diesel locomotive, No. 265031, coupled behind, possibly to be used for shunting at the terminal point.

No. 155020, 24 July 2015

No. 155020 passes through Hamburg-Harburg light engine. Built by LEW Hennigsdorf, 273 of these locomotives were built from 1974 onwards, and they were used in both East and West Germany.

No. 155036, 24 July 2015

No. 155036 passes through Hamburg-Harburg with a container working from the nearby docks. An unusual feature of this class is the horn on the front of the cab, which points downwards.

No. 155048, 21 July 2015

No. 155048 passes Düsseldorf-Rath with a loaded automotive working. Some Class 155 locomotives are now starting to be withdrawn and sold to private operators for further use.

No. 155055, 24 July 2015

No. 155055 passes Hamburg-Harburg with a container working. This locomotive doesn't carry the DB logo on the cab front like the majority of its classmates.

No. 155239, 23 July 2015

No. 155239 departs from the large yard adjacent to Hannover Linden Fischerhof with a rake of empty cartic wagons. When delivered to East Germany, this class of locomotive was the most powerful to run in that side of the country.

No. 181204, 6 May 2016

No. 181204 is seen stabled in between duties at Basel Badischer Bahnhof. Class 181 locomotives were built for cross-border traffic between Germany and Luxembourg, and were able to run off two different voltages. (TC)

No. 182024, 24 July 2015

No. 182024 passes Hamburg-Harburg while hauling a rake of single-deck carriages. There are twenty-five of this type of locomotive in service, which are very similar to the Class 152 locomotives, but have the Taurus body design.

No. 185083, 21 July 2015

No. 185083 is seen passing Düsseldorf-Rath with an intermodal working. This class of locomotive is part of the Bombardier TRAXX family of locomotives, which can be seen all over Continental Europe.

No. 185102, 9 September 2014

No. 185102 is seen passing Basel Badischer Bahnhof with a freight working, which is typical of the class, as these locomotives can be seen hauling freights in various different countries across Europe.

No. 185106, 10 September 2014

No. 185106 is seen at Erstfeld, Switzerland, having arrived with a freight working double-headed with classmate No. 185120. The locomotives have just traversed the Gotthard route, and No. 185106 will detach here in the yard to allow No. 185120 to continue solo. Most freight now uses the Gotthard Base Tunnel.

No. 185113, 10 September 2014

No. 185113 is seen at Chiasso, on the Swiss-Italian border, waiting to take over a freight working that has originated in Italy. The locos will work the train over the arduous Gotthard route to Erstfeld, where the leading loco, No. 185091, will detach, allowing No. 185113 to continue solo.

No. 185126, 9 September 2014

No. 185126 rushes through Rheinfelden, Switzerland, with a rake of cargowaggons. Rheinfelden is situated near Basel, in the far north of Switzerland.

No. 185127, 9 September 2014

No. 185127 is seen passing through Pratteln, Switzerland, with a rake of cargowaggons. This station is not far from the large marshalling yard at Muttenz, just outside Basel, and is a very busy location.

No. 185215, 20 April 2016

No. 185215 is seen running through Wels, Austria, with a loaded timber working. The Class 185 TRAXX locomotives are equipped to work in various other European locations, not just Germany, and can be seen regularly working away from their home country.

No. 185239, 20 April 2016

No. 185239 is seen approaching St Polten station in Austria at the head of a freight working. The remains of the former Railion logos can be seen underneath the DB logo on the bodyside.

No. 185282, 22 July 2015

No. 185282 is seen passing Köln West while working in tandem with classmate No. 185310. Both locos carry different logos on the bodyside, with No. 185310 still retaining the old Railion logos and No. 185282 carrying DB logos.

No. 185325, 29 April 2014

No. 185325 is seen passing through Kolding station in Denmark at the head of a mixed freight heading back towards Germany. This locomotive, which was one of a batch of TRAXX locos that operated into Scandinavia for DB Cargo, has the silver Green Cargo cabsides.

No. 185331, 24 July 2015

No. 185331 passes through Hamburg-Harburg at the head of a freight working. This is another Class 185 that operated into Denmark at the time, and it also has the Green Cargo logos applied.

No. 185334, 24 July 2015

No. 185334 is seen passing Hamburg-Harburg with an intermodal working, heading for the docks. This is one of the Class 185 locomotives that operate in Denmark, and those that do have Green Cargo logos on the cabside.

No. 185369, 20 February 2017

No. 185369 runs through Wuppertal at the head of a mixed freight working along with classmate No. 185289. This class often run in pairs on the heavier freights through the country. (TC)

No. 186340, 4 November 2017

No. 186340 is seen stabled at Antwerpen-Noord Depot in the Netherlands. The Class 186 is a dual voltage version of the Class 185 locomotives, being able to operate under both AC and DC currents. No. 186340 works under the Euro Cargo Rail banner.

No. 189045, 21 July 2015

No. 189045 works through Düsseldorf-Rath in tandem with classmate No. 189041 at the head of a heavy ore train. The locomotives that work these trains are fitted with autocouplers, as can be seen on the front of No. 189045.

No. 189059, 24 July 2015

No. 189059 passes through Hamburg-Harburg with an intermodal working heading for the nearby docks. The Class 189 locomotives are part of the Siemens Eurosprinter locomotive family, and are also known as Class ES 64 F4.

No. 189076, 1 May 2017

No. 189076 is seen standing on the through lines at Roosendaal in the Netherlands with a rake of loaded cartic wagons. This class of locomotive is another than can be seen working in different Europe countries, not just Germany.

No. 189085, 22 July 2015

No. 189085 runs light engine past Köln West as an ore working travels in the opposite direction. The Class 189 locomotives are also popular with private operators in Germany, not just with DB Cargo.

No. 204605, 12 March 2018

No. 204605 is seen acting as yard pilot at Pirdop in Bulgaria. Originally designated Class V100s, over 1,100 of this type of locomotive were built from 1966 onwards, operating all over Germany. Many have now been withdrawn, while some are still active as yard pilots.

No. 218307, 24 July 2015

No. 218307 runs light engine through Hamburg HBF. This class of locomotives was built as mixed traffic locos from 1971 onwards, and totaled nearly 400 examples, along with a pre-production batch of prototypes. Many are still in use on passenger turns, although they are rapidly diminishing.

No. 218359, 13 May 2016

No. 218359 is seen being hauled light engine through Hamburg HBF by a classmate. A lot of the Class 218 locomotives seen at Hamburg are allocated to Niebüll Depot. (TC)

No. 218474, 13 May 2016

No. 218474 runs light engine through Hamburg-Harburg wearing a very faded DB livery. Of note is the S-Bahn Hamburg logo on the bodyside. (TC)

No. 218812, 23 July 2015

No. 218812 is seen stabled at Hannover HBF, awaiting its next turn of duty. The main production batch of this class was built by four different manufacturers over an eight-year period during the 1970s, and there were twelve prototypes built in 1971.

No. 232131, 21 July 2015

No. 232131 is seen having arrived at Düsseldorf-Rath with a freight working. The October Revolution Locomotive Works, at their Voroshilovgrad Works in Luhansk, Ukraine, built over 700 of these locomotives in the Soviet Union during the 1970s.

No. 232469, 24 July 2015

No. 232469 leans into the curve at Hamburg-Harburg with a loaded container working. This class was originally built for the German Democratic Republic, but with reunification their use spread to all over Germany.

No. 232669, 24 July 2015

No. 232669 works past Hamburg-Harburg while in tandem with classmate No. 233698, at the head of an intermodal working. This class have been nicknamed 'Ludmillas', and other similar locomotives were built for use in Bulgaria, the Czech Republic, Slovakia and the USSR.

No. 233306, 24 July 2015

No. 233306 passes Hamburg-Harburg with a rake of cargowaggons. The Class 233 locomotives differed from the main production batch of Class 232 locomotives in that they were equipped with a different type of Kolomna engine.

No. 261027, 24 July 2015

No. 261027 trundles light engine through Hamburg-Harburg on its way to the nearby docks. This class of locomotive were built by Voith, and form part of their Gravita family of engines. DB have two different types of this locomotive in use; namely, Class 261s and Class 265s.

No. 261105, 21 July 2015

No. 261105 is seen in use as yard pilot at Düsseldorf-Rath. These locomotives are used as yard pilots and can also be seen at the head of trip workings, which are still seen in large numbers in Germany.

No. 265022, 21 July 2015

No. 265022 works through Düsseldorf-Rath with a train of loaded steel coils. The Class 265 Gravita locomotives are a more powerful version of the Class 261 locomotives.

No. 294674, 24 July 2015

Hauling No. 295019, No. 294674 runs light engine through Hamburg-Harburg. The Class 294 locomotives were originally part of the large Class 290 family of locomotives, but they were renumbered into the Class 294 series upon the fitting of remote control equipment.

No. 294845, 22 July 2015

No. 294845 runs through Köln West while hauling small shunter No. 363824. This locomotive still carries its former Railion logos and has yet to have DB logos applied.

No. 295019, 24 July 2015

No. 295019 passes through Hamburg-Harburg while being hauled by No. 294674. The Class 295 locomotives were renumbered from Class 291 locos when they were fitted with autocouplers and remote control equipment.

No. 295044, 24 July 2015

Renumbered from 291044, No. 295044 is seen running light engine past Hamburg-Harburg. The autocoupler can be seen in the raised position on the front.

No. 295054, 24 July 2015

No. 295054 is also seen running light engine through Hamburg-Harburg, this time heading towards the dock complex. There is still a considerable requirement in Germany for large pilot and trip locomotives.

No. 362423, 23 February 2017

No. 362423 is seen while employed on station pilot duty at Stralsund Bahnhof, positioning locomotive No. 101074 onto its train. (TC)

No. 362448, 23 July 2015

No. 362448 is seen stabled in between pilot duties at Hannover HBF. Over 1,000 of these shunters were built from the mid-1950s onwards, and were originally designated as Class V60. The Class 362 locomotives have been refurbished with Caterpillar engines and are also fitted with remote control equipment.

No. 363810, 24 July 2015

No. 363810 runs light engine through Hamburg-Harburg. The Class 363 locomotives are a heavier and larger version of the Class 362 locomotives.

No. 363824, 22 July 2015

No. 363824 is seen being hauled light engine through Köln West by the much larger No. 294845. The Class 363 locomotives are also fitted with autocouplers, as can be seen.

No. 363830, 24 July 2015

No. 363830 is seen negotiating the myriad of lines and junctions at Hamburg HBF, while employed on station pilot duty. There are still hundreds of these locos in use, dotted all over the country.

Private Operators

No. 37026, 22 July 2015

No. 37026 runs light engine through Köln West. Despite carrying full SNCF Fret livery, this loco is operated by Akiem, and is one of sixty locomotives that were built by Alstom as part of their Prima family of locomotives.

No. 139135, 11 May 2016

No. 139135 is seen on one of the through roads at Innsbruck station, Austria. This class of loco dates from the mid-1950s and most of the DB examples have been withdrawn, with Lokomotion (LM) operating eight examples in their distinctive livery, as seen here. (TC)

No. 140761, 23 July 2015

No. 140761 is seen passing through Bremen HBF with a rake of loaded cartic wagons. This loco was retired by DB and was later purchased by Mittelweserbahn (MWB), in whose livery it is seen.

No. 140857, 24 July 2015

No. 140857 passes Hamburg-Harburg with a container working. The sheer amount of traffic generated by the docks in Hamburg is incredible. There still some Class 140 locomotives in use with DB, but others are now starting to appear with private operators, including No. 140857, which is run by Eisenbahngesellschaft Potsdam (EGP).

No. 140870, 23 July 2015

No. 140870 passes through Bremen HBF with a rake of empty cartic wagons. This loco was retired from DB use and is now operated by Eisenbahnen Und Verkehrsbetriebe Elbe-Weser (EVB).

No. 140876, 24 July 2015

No. 140876 runs through Hamburg-Harburg, heading for the docks. This loco still retains its old DB red livery, but is now operated by Eisenbahngesellschaft Potsdam (EGP).

No. 143063, 24 July 2015

No. 143063 passes through Hamburg-Harburg along with classmate No. 143217. Both of these locomotives were retired by DB and were bought by RBH Logistics (RBH), in whose attractive livery they are seen. Both carry RBH numbers, numbered 107 and 126 respectively. RBH operate a large number of these locomotives on heavy oil trains.

No. 143851, 23 July 2015

No. 143851 passes through Hannover Linden Fischerhof with a rake of covered cartic wagons. Class 143 locomotives have been heavily used on passenger traffic by DB over the years, but their duties are diminishing, and some locomotives have been sold to private operators, including No. 143851, which is now operated by Mitteldeutsche Braunkohlengesellschaft (MEG), numbered 603.

No. 143864, 24 July 2015

No. 143864 is seen being hauled through Hamburg-Harburg by classmate No. 143310. Both locomotives are operated by Mitteldeutsche Braunkohlengesellschaft, numbered 606 and 607 respectively.

No. 145087, 24 July 2015

No. 145087 passes through Hamburg-Harburg with a container working from the docks. This loco is one of several Class 145s in private use, being operated by SRI Rail Invest (SRI) and carrying the name *Barbara*. The SRI livery is certainly very pleasing on the eye.

No. 145094, 24 July 2015

No. 145094 is seen passing through Hamburg-Harburg with a loaded container working. This loco is part of a small batch of privately operated Class 145 locomotives, in this case being operated by Captrain (CAPT).

No. 146501, 24 July 2015

No. 146501 is seen departing Hamburg-Harburg with a passenger working to Uelzen. Metronom operate local service around Hamburg, as far afield as Bremen, using Class 146 TRAXX locomotives. No. 146501 carries the Metronom number 146-01 and the name *Scheebel*.

No. 146502, 23 July 2015

No. 146502 arrives at Bremen HBF carrying Metronom livery, but also an advert for Niedersachsen Ticket. This loco also carries the Metronom number 146-02 and the name *Hansestadt Lüneburg*.

No. 146541, 24 July 2015

No. 146541 is seen arriving at Hamburg-Harburg with a Metronom passenger working. This particular loco carries unbranded livery and has the full running number on the front instead of the usual Metronom number.

No. 151033, 13 May 2016

No. 151033 passes through Hamburg-Harburg with a container working. The amount of traffic through this station is phenomenal, with there being a procession of freight workings throughout the day, and also a large variety of passenger turns as well. No. 151033 carries the livery of operator Eisenbahngesellschaft Potsdam (EGP). (TC)

No. 151060, 11 May 2016

No. 151060 is seen at Brenner station on the Italian-Austrian border, which passes through the Alps. This is a very busy rail link between the two countries, with large amounts of traffic passing through. No. 151060 is seen still carrying its former DB red livery, but was in fact operated by Lokomotion (LM) by this time. (TC)

No. 151152, 4 May 2016

No. 151152 passes through Trier station while working in multiple with a classmate. A total of 170 Class 151 locomotives were in use with DB, but a start has been made into withdrawing and selling them on to other operators. Both locomotives in this view are now operated by RBH Logistics (RBH), in whose livery No. 151152 is seen. It also carries their number 262. (TC)

No. 152197, 24 July 2015

No. 152197 passes Hamburg-Harburg with a container service, heading for the docks. This is one of only two Class 152 locomotives in private use, both of which are operated by Import Transport Logistik Eisenbahngesellschaft (ITL).

No. 182509, 24 July 2015

No. 182509 departs from Hamburg HBF with an HKX passenger working to Köln HBF. This Taurus loco is one of many that are operated by Dispolok and are hired out to various different operators. These passenger workings are now known as FlixTrain.

No. 182534, 13 May 2016

No. 182534 departs from Hamburg-Harburg while hauling a rake of single-deck carriages on another of the HKX workings from Hamburg, heading for Köln. This Taurus locomotive is owned by Dispolok, and is one of many on the Continent hired out to other operators, both on passenger and freight workings. (TC)

No. 182912, 24 July 2015

No. 182912 passes through Hamburg-Harburg with a loaded container working. This Taurus locomotive belongs to the Siemens-built Eurosprinter family of locomotives, which are popular all across Europe, especially in Austria. No. 182912 is operated by Mittelweserbahn (MWB).

No. 183717, 20 April 2016

No. 183717 is seen running round its freight working at Wels station in Austria. This Taurus locomotive is operated by Steiermarkbahn Transport und Logistik (STBAT), and is seen in their distinctive livery.

No. 185532, 22 July 2015

No. 185532 passes through Köln West with a loaded container working. The Class 185 locomotives that are operated by private companies are numbered from 185501 upwards. No. 185532 is another locomotive operated by Captrain (CAPT).

No. 185544, 23 July 2015

No. 185544 passes through one of the platform roads at Bremen HBF while hauling a rake of covered car-carrying wagons. Bremen is a fantastic place to spend some time, with vast amounts of both DB and private freight workings to be seen. No. 185544 is operated by Dispolok (DISPO).

No. 185556, 13 May 2016

TRAXX locomotive No. 185556 passes Hamburg-Harburg with a container working while carrying the distinctive black livery of owner Dispolok. At the time it was on hire to Rhenus Logistics (HHLA), and it carries their logo on the front cab. Dispolok was a locomotive leasing company set up by Siemens, but it became part of the Mitsui Group, hence the MRCE logo also on the front of the cab. (TC)

No. 185586, 13 May 2016

No. 185586 runs through Hamburg-Harburg along with a Dispolok-liveried Class 189 locomotive at the head of an oil train. This TRAXX locomotive was operated by RheinCargo (RHC), but it also carries the identity of former operator Häfen und Güterverkehr (HGK), as well as their number, 2054. Certain locomotives tend to have different operators' liveries when they are leased out. (TC)

No. 185599, 21 July 2015

No. 185599 passes through Köln West with an intermodal working. At the time this locomotive was operated by Crossrail (XRAIL), but since this shot was taken the locomotive has a new owner, HSL Logistik (HSL).

No. 185615, 23 July 2015

No. 185615 works an empty steel working through the centre roads at Bremen HBF. This is another Class 185 TRAXX locomotive that carries the base colour for the Bombardier-built locos, and this particular loco is operated by Verkehrsbetriebe Peine-Salzgitter (VPS).

No. 185618, 21 July 2015

No. 185618 passes through Düsseldorf-Rath with an oil working. This TRAXX locomotive is operated by RheinCargo (RHC) and carries the base livery for TRAXX locomotives delivered by Bombardier – a livery that is similar to the SNCB-operated locomotives.

No. 185630, 21 July 2015

No. 185630 is seen running light engine through Düsseldorf-Rath. This is another of the popular TRAXX locomotives, and this particular example carries the livery of former operator Häfen und Güterverkehr (HGK), as well as their number 2065, but by this time is was in use with RheinCargo (RHC).

No. 185663, 11 May 2016

No. 185663 is seen at the very picturesque Innsbruck station, in Austria. This German-registered Class 185 TRAXX locomotive is operated by Lokomotion (LM), and is seen with a fellow LM locomotive No. 139135. German-registered locomotives can be seen far and wide all over Europe, not just in Germany. (TC)

No. 186200, 22 July 2015

No. 186200 passes light engine through Köln West while hauling classmate No. 186218. Both locomotives are operated by Belgian National operator SNCB, and both carry green and grey livery. They also carry Belgian running numbers, being 2808 and 2826 respectively. The 'E' before the running number indicates the locomotives can operate in Italy.

No. 186237, 23 July 2015

No. 186237 departs the yard at Hannover Linden Fischerhof with an oil working. It is operated by Logistik Und Transport (LTE) and is another Bombardier-built TRAXX locomotive, a type widely used on the Continent.

No. 186442, 11 May 2016

No. 186442 is seen at the head of an intermodal working at Bolzano in Northern Italy. The Class 186 locomotives are also seen far and wide across Europe, with No. 186442 registered to German operator Lokomotion (LM). (TC)

No. 189098, 22 July 2015

No. 189098 passes through Köln West with a loaded container working. The privately operated Class 189 locomotives are numbered starting from 189090, and No. 189098 is operated by Dispolok, but in this view was on hire to Locon Logistik Und Consulting (LOCON).

No. 189203, 22 July 2015

No. 189203 passes through Köln West while hauling classmate No. 189102 dead in tow. The two locos carry different liveries, but are both owned by Dispolok, with them being leased to different operators – No. 189203 to European Rail Shuttle Railways (ERS) and No. 189102 to Swiss National operator SBB Cargo.

No. 189821, 24 July 2015

No. 189821 is seen also passing through Hamburg-Harburg with a container working towards the docks. The Class 189 locomotives are popular with private operators and are part of the Siemens Eurosprinter family of locomotives. No. 189821 is operated by Locon Logistik Und Consulting (LOCON) and carries the name *LOCON 502*.

No. 193219, 22 July 2015

No. 193219 is seen passing through Köln West with an intermodal working. This Vectron, like many others, is operated by the European Locomotive Leasing Company, who hire them out to other operators, with No. 193219 being used by Osthannoversche Eisenbahnen (OHE Cargo).

No. 193609, 13 May 2016

No. 193609 is seen passing through Hamburg-Harburg light engine along with a classmate. This type of locomotive is known as a Vectron, and they are starting to appear in vast numbers all over Continental Europe, with many different types able to operate under different voltages. This particular locomotive is owned by Dispolok (DISPO), and also carries the number X4 E-609 on the front. (TC)

No. 193842, 24 July 2015

No. 193842 heads through Hamburg-Harburg with a loaded container working, heading for the docks. This Vectron locomotive is operated by boxXpress (BOX). The Vectron family of locomotives is becoming increasingly common all over Continental Europe.

No. 193861, 23 July 2015

No. 193861 is seen departing from the yard near Hannover Linden Fischerhof with a loaded container working. This Vectron is operated by Dispolok, and is on hire to boxXpress, carrying their logo.

No. 193876, 23 July 2015

No. 193876 glides through Bremen HBF with a rake of covered car-carrying wagons. This loco is operated by Dispolok (DISPO) and is seen carrying a special twenty-five-year livery made up of jigsaw pieces.

No. 199014, 22 February 2017

No. 199014 *Otto* is seen stabled at Bad Doberan on the Molli Railway. This railway is a preserved narrow gauge line located near Mecklenburg. There are four of these diesel locomotives operated by the line. (TC)

No. 203001, 24 July 2015

No. 203001 passes light engine through Hamburg-Harburg. Many shunting locomotives found use with private operators after finishing with DB, with No. 203001 being no exception; it is operated by SG Lubeck (SGL), in whose plain white livery it is seen.

No. 203155, 22 July 2015

No. 203155 passes through Köln West at the head on oil working. This loco is operated by Alstom Lokomotiven Services (ALS), and confusingly carries their number 203443.

No. 203160, 11 August 2015

No. 203160 is seen at Amersfoort in the Netherlands. Despite being used in the Netherlands, it is registered in Germany.

No. 203166, 13 May 2016

No. 203166 passes through Hamburg-Harburg with an empty flat wagon. Another example of a shunting and trip locomotive finding use after DB, this particular locomotive is operated by STRABAG. (TC)

No. 204373, 13 May 2016

No. 204373 passes through Hamburg-Harburg with a container working. This locomotive is now operated by Locon Logistik Und Consulting (LOCON) and carries the name *LOCON 203*. (TC)

No. 212052, 22 July 2015

No. 212052 is seen passing through Köln West, being hauled by No. 225023 while on a departmental working. Over 380 of these locomotives were built and all of the ones left running are in private hands. No. 212052 is operated by EfW-Verkehrsgesellschaft (EfW).

No. 223012, 20 April 2016

No. 223012 passes through Wels, Austria, while carrying Dispolok livery. This loco is a part of the Siemens Eurorunner family, and is similar to the Austrian OBB Class 2016 Hercules locomotives. No. 223012 is operated by Beacon Rail Leasing (BRLL), and is German-registered.

No. 223031, 24 July 2015

No. 223031 passes Hamburg-Harburg while double-heading with No. 275101. No. 223031 is a Siemens-built Eurorunner type locomotive, very similar to the Austrian Class 2016 Hercules locomotives, and is operated by Eisenbahnen Und Verkehrsbetriebe Elbe-Weser (EVB).

No. 225023, 22 July 2015

No. 225023 passes through Köln West with a departmental working, with No. 212052 in tow. Both of these locomotives are operated by EfW-Verkehrsgesellschaft (EfW), and No. 225023 still carries DB livery, but with new logos.

No. 225099, 22 July 2015

No. 225099 passes through Köln West with ballast working formed of railpro two-axle wagons. This loco is operated by BBL Logistik (BBL), and was one of sixty-eight renumbered from DB Class 215s.

No. 241002, 24 July 2015

No. 241002 passes Hamburg-Harburg with an intermodal working, operated by HectorRail. The Class 241 locomotives operated by this Swedish-based operator are part of the Bombardier TRAXX family of locos, and HectorRail operate between Sweden and Germany via Denmark. No. 241002 is named *Skywalker*.

No. 246005, 24 July 2015

No. 246005 is seen at Hamburg-Harburg, waiting to depart for Hamburg HBF. The Class 246 locomotives are a diesel version of the popular Class 146 TRAXX locomotives, built by Bombardier. No. 246005 carries the name *Horneburg*.

No. 261302, 22 July 2015

No. 261302 passes light engine through Köln West. Built by Voith, this loco is part of their Gravita family of locomotives and is operated by Northrail (NRAIL). Northrail operate three of these locomotives, and they are similar to the DB Cargo Class 261 engines.

No. 261310, 22 July 2015

No. 261310 is seen at Köln West, hauling a rake of covered steel wagons. This is another Voith Gravita locomotive operated by Northrail (NRAIL), and is seen carrying their attractive orange livery.

No. 263004, 13 May 2016

No. 263004 passes light engine through Hamburg-Harburg. These hugely impressive locomotives were built by Voith and are part of their Maxima Class of locomotives. There are just thirteen of the Maxima 30CC locomotives in use, all with private operators. (TC)

No. 263005, 13 May 2016

No. 263005 passes through Hamburg-Harburg, being hauled by No. 265500. There are two different versions of the Maxima locomotive in use; the Class 263 locomotives are the less powerful versions, with the Class 264 having larger engines. (TC)

No. 265500, 13 May 2016

No. 265500 passes through Hamburg-Harburg while hauling No. 263005. Both locomotives are registered to Voith Transport (VTLT), and No. 265500 is part of the Gravita Class of locomotives, of which Voith operate three. (TC)

No. 266015, 24 July 2015

No. 266015 passes Hamburg-Harburg with a rake of bogie aggregate wagons. This loco carries the attractive livery of Heavy Haul Power International (HHPI), as well as the name *Rhoda Painter* and number 29003.

No. 266029, 23 July 2015

No. 266029 approaches Bremen HBF with a freight working while carrying a different Heavy Haul Power International (HHPI) livery. It also carries a name, *Ted Gaffney*, and the HHPI number 29005.

No. 266037, 24 July 2015

No. 266037 passes through Hamburg-Harburg with a ballast working. This loco is operated by Dispolok (DISPO), but also carries the number MRCE 513-10 on the cab front.

No. 266042, 13 May 2016

No. 266042 passes through Hamburg-Harburg with a ballast working. This General Motors-built JT42CWR locomotive is one of many hundreds that can be seen all over Europe, including the UK, where they are better known as Class 66s. No. 266042 is registered to Beacon Rail Locomotive Leasing (BRLL), but also carries the number MRCE 561-5. (TC)

No. 266063, 13 May 2016

No. 266063 passes through Hamburg-Harburg with a ballast working. With many private operators applying their own numbers, this loco displays the number PB04 on the front, as well as having to carry its official twelve-digit European number. (TC)

No. 266120, 1 May 2017

No. 266120 is seen stabled at Roosendaal in the Netherlands. This locomotive is one of many Class 66 type locos in use in Europe, and No. 266120 is owned by Beacon Rail Leasing (BRLL), being hired out to various different operators.

No. 272012, 22 July 2015

No. 272012 runs light engine through Köln West. This locomotive was built by MAK and is one of just twenty-four locomotives built to this design, with the majority now being operated by RheinCargo (RHC), including No. 272012. The loco carries the livery of former operator Häfen und Güterverkehr (HGK), as well as their number, DE74.

No. 272015, 22 July 2015

No. 272015 trundles through Köln West with a local trip working consisting of two bogie tank wagons and two open barrier vehicles. This is another example of the MAK-built DE 1002 locomotives operated by RheinCargo still carrying Häfen und Güterverkehr (HGK) livery and also their number, which is DE76.

No. 272018, 22 July 2015

No. 272018 is seen passing through Köln West while hauling a rake of bogie tank wagons. Köln West is an excellent place to see these RheinCargo (RHC)-operated locomotives, as there are large numbers of local trip workings that these are employed on. Still carrying Häfen und Güterverkehr (HGK) livery, it also carries their number, DE92.

No. 272020, 22 July 2015

No. 272020 is seen passing Köln West with a small rake of large bulk powder wagons. The variety of different traffic types in Germany is incredible, although the majority, like most countries, is intermodal container traffic. No. 272020 still carries Häfen und Güterverkehr (HGK) livery, and also carries their number DE82.

No. 274108, 21 July 2015

No. 274108 is seen while shunting at Düsseldorf-Rath. This locomotive is part of the Vossloh/MAK-built G1205 series of locomotives, and this particular loco is operated by Teutoburger Wald Eisenbahngesellschaft (TWE), though it is carrying Captrain livery and Captrain number V157.

No. 275018, 21 July 2015

No. 275018 is seen passing through Düsseldorf-Rath at the head of a rake of bulk hoppers. This locomotive was built by Vossloh and is one of their G1206 locomotives, which can be seen in great numbers in Germany on trip and shunt workings. No. 275018 is operated by Niederrheinische Verkehrsbetriebe (NIAG) and carries their number 7.

No. 275019, 21 July 2015

No. 275019 passes Köln West at the head of an oil working. This type of train is operated in Germany in large numbers. Operated by Northrail (NRAIL), this loco is another example of the Vossloh-built G1206 Class.

No. 275021, 22 July 2015

No. 275021 runs light engine through Köln West. This is another Vossloh-built G1206, and there are numerous examples with private operators all over Germany. No. 275021 is operated by Duisport Rail (DPR).

No. 277809, 13 May 2016

No. 277809 passes through Hamburg-Harburg with a container working. Yet another Vossloh-built locomotive, this is part of the G1700 Class of locomotive, and is seen being operated by Max Bögl Bauunternehmung (MBBAU), but it was formerly operated by Neuss-Düsseldorfer Häfen GmbH (NE). (TC)

No. 285113, 22 July 2015

No. 285113 is seen passing through Köln West with a rake of bulk powder wagons. This loco is operated by RheinCargo (RHC) and carries their number DE802. No. 285113 is a diesel version of the popular TRAXX family of locomotives, and was built by Bombardier in 2007.

No. 293005, 13 May 2016

No. 293005 passes through Hamburg-Harburg with a ballast working. This loco carries the very distinctive black livery of SES Logistik (SES) and was rebuilt from loco No. 201833 by Alstom in 2001. It also carries the name *Georg*, which can be seen at the far end of the loco. (TC)

No. 352002, 13 May 2016

No. 352002 passes through Hamburg-Harburg with a rake of empty wagons. This loco was built by Vossloh in 1974 and is one of their G320B locomotives. There are currently just four of these working in Germany, with Northrail operating a pair. No. 352002 carries the distinctive Northrail (NRAIL) orange livery. (TC)

No. 363698, 24 February 2017

No. 363698 is seen stabled at Putbus. This shunter is preserved and is owned by Eisenbahn-Bau- und Betriebsgesellschaft Pressnitztalbahn mbH (PRESS) company, who run between Bergen and Lauterbach Mole. The loco carries the number 363029, but is in fact No. 363698. (TC)

No. 386012, 23 July 2015

No. 386012 passes through Bremen HBF with a container working. Metrans are based in the Czech Republic and use their own locomotives all the way from Prague to Rotterdam in the Netherlands via Germany. The Class 386s are a version of the TRAXX locomotive.

No. 482042, 23 July 2015

No. 482042 is seen at Bremen HBF on one of the through roads while hauling an oil train. This loco is operated by Swiss National operator SBB Cargo, but like the majority of the class it is hired out to different operators. The loco also carries Railpool logos at the far end.

Acknowledgements

A very big thank you goes to Tony Cole, who provided some invaluable photographs; those marked (TC) are credited to him. Thank you also to Matt Parker for providing valuable assistance on the passenger side of the workings in Germany.

No. 187302, 14 May 2018

No.187302 is seen waiting for a path through Wien Hauptbahnhof, Austria. This Class 187 loco is operated by Railpool (RPOOL), in whose livery it is seen. The Class 187 locomotives are part of TRAXX Last Mile locomotives and have a small diesel engine, and can also run off the overhead wires.